Volume 109 of the Yale Series of Younger Poets

T0366633

ANSEL ELKINS

Blue Yodel

FOREWORD BY CARL PHILLIPS

Yale UNIVERSITY PRESS

NEW HAVEN AND LONDON

Published with assistance from a grant to honor James Merrill and
with assistance from the Louis Stern Memorial Fund.

Yale University Press books may be purchased in quantity for
educational, business, or promotional use. For information, please
e-mail sales.press@yale.edu (U.S. office) or sales@yaleup.co.uk (U.K.
office).

Set in Janson Oldstyle type by Tseng Information Systems, Inc.
Printed and bound by CPI Group (UK) Ltd, Croydon, CR0 4YY
Library of Congress Cataloging-in-Publication Data
Elkins, Ansel, 1982–
[Poems. Selections]
Blue yodel / Ansel Elkins ; foreword by Carl Phillips.
pages cm. — (Yale series of younger poets; volume 109)
ISBN 978-0-300-21003-3 (cloth : alk. paper) —
ISBN 978-0-300-21002-6 (pbk. : alk. paper)
I. Title.
PS3605.L417A6 2015
811′.6—dc23   2014031909

10 9 8 7 6 5 4 3 2 1

To Scarlett Saavedra
and
Ken Elkins,

who gave me life and taught me joy

A pair of eyes was painted on my cheeks as a sign
that I could see in more ways than one.

—Zora Neale Hurston

Contents

Foreword

"In this land, lost/things just happen/to be found," says one of Ansel
Elkins's speakers, and indeed, *Blue Yodel* is everywhere populated
with the lost (a murdered wife, a girl ripped from her mother's grasp
by a tornado), those who half desire to *be* lost (a wife stuck in the rut
of monogamy, another woman whose "body's unbridled/appetite"
lures her "like a hunter into the animal night"), and those whose
very being has exiled them from the realm too often referred to
as normal (a girl with antlers, a wounder and captor of an angel, a
sailor whose wife, quite literally, is his ship—to name but a few). In
"Mississippi Pastoral," what "just happen[s] / to be found" is a dead
black boy:

> A seventy-five pound
> cotton gin fan
> strung with barbed wire
>
> leashed to the child's neck. Swollen
> August sun, white blaze. Today
> the cotton fields set themselves on fire.

The coolness—the casualness—with which Elkins juxtaposes
the grisly murder and the southern landscape (its heat, its light) is
chilling. As it turns out, this kind of juxtapositioning characterizes
almost all of the poems in *Blue Yodel* and in Elkins's hands proves
itself a powerful strategy for instruction, if it can be instructive—as
I believe it can—to raise in a reader more questions than answers in
the face of conundrum. Here is Elkins's "Goat Man":

Like a bearded prophet out of the Old Testament
he travels through our county roads on foot
with his iron-wheeled wagon drawn by a herd
of thirty goats, the solitary music of trembling
tinware, beaten pails and kettles.
In the slash pine, children gather to see
him preach the Gospel. He lectures on God,
politics, and women. He says he was in Alabama
last week, and warns of the coming
race wars. Afterward he sold us postcards,
let us pet a newborn kid before we left for home.
In winter nights the goats sleep close; he heats
his supper over a fire of burning tires
and reads *Robinson Crusoe* in the intimate field
of light afforded by a kerosene lamp.
He nails his hand-painted sign to a live oak
by the roadside: GOD IS NOT DEAD. He rises
at first bird when the sun surfaces behind a hill.
We can hear the sound of bells carried
by his goats, their curved regal horns
breaking a path through the morning chill
of the Old Dixie highway where he walks
on the fresh-laid tar of the mid-twentieth century.

Who is this man? Simply—and not so simply—what he appears to
be, Elkins suggests: a preacher and a man who doesn't herd goats but
whose wagon is drawn by a herd of goats; a reader of *Robinson Crusoe;*

and a figure who seems to straddle the Old Testament of the poem's
beginning and the Old Dixie with which it ends (or almost ends,
before Old Dixie morphs into a highway that, in turn, morphs into
the mid-twentieth century—again, via juxtaposition). Are we meant
to align the Old South with the Old Testament, then? If so, does that
suggest that the South is antiquated, a decided throwback, or does
it somehow retain, along with the mystery of the Old Testament,
some of the Old Testament's timelessness and grandeur? Is that
why the colloquialism of rising "at first bird" gets quickly followed
by the transformation of the goats from the homely creatures they
are to something loftier (more biblical?), "their curved regal horns/
breaking a path through the morning chill"? And what of the odd
moment that seems almost accidentally tossed in, where for two
lines we encounter a specific past tense event in a poem otherwise
governed by the present tense:

> Afterward he sold us postcards,
> let us pet a newborn kid before we left for home.

These lines, thanks to the first person and to the sudden shift to past
tense, make a space for intimacy and for particularity; they offer
a specific incident that occurred within the ongoing present of the
goat man's passage across a landscape. They suggest at least part of
how he makes a living (selling postcards), but also a tenderness of
sorts, insofar as he cares for a newborn goat and lets the speakers
(children? adults?) pet it. But if this man does indeed straddle
the Old Testament and Old Dixie, how does tenderness figure?

Tenderness is hardly what the Old Testament brings to mind. And it is difficult to consider tenderness side by side with an Old Dixie soon to be fraught with "the coming / race wars" (about which, notice, the goat man warns without ever saying which side of those wars he might be on).

Again, the strategy for generating these questions lies in juxtaposition and how it invites us to make unexpected associations. This occurs not just within individual poems but in the book's sequencing of the poems. "Thou Shalt Not," for example—a poem whose suggestion of how no should have meant no (but didn't) conjures the idea of rape—is immediately followed by "The Call of the Wild," wherein a woman recalls her lusting for a man ("Every line out of my mouth is a lie/except the one that begins with *I want*"). This is followed in turn by a poem in which a girl, having been warned against the seduction of wolves, deliberately goes "into the night woods, where she whispers/*Wolf! Come find me.*" And the poem right after it is "Going to the Movies Alone," in which a man starts out confessing his desire to see mass destruction on-screen, then seems to confess to a desire to be a mass murderer himself.

What to make of this sequencing? We're asked, implicitly, to consider rape next to female desire, and to consider that particular desire next to a desire for mass destruction, which, like rape, is a form of violation. Rape is unwanted violation. But to desire violation can be a healthy enough sexual behavior, between consenting adults. The desire to randomly violate a group of people—as in mass murder—doesn't involve consenting adults. Why, then, do all three behaviors seem uneasily related? Because

Elkins groups them together, and our human instinct is to reach for pattern and to impose it where we cannot find it. In this way, I think Elkins means to create questions in her readers that deliberately make them uncomfortable. She wants to disturb us from any easy assumptions and leave us in a place where we might not ever arrive at a conclusion, but we'll have come to understand that most of life is a lot more complex than we might want to believe.

"I want to tear through the border between dream and reality," says Elkins's would-be mass murderer, who goes on to detail the various forms of violence he longs for, before exiting the theater:

> I clear the frost from my window,
> try to unlock the frozen door.

That's how the poem ends. Without moral conclusion. We've been shown a certain unattractive sensibility, then we're left with an image of this man as any other person on the street—which most of the worst criminals in fact are, until they show themselves to be otherwise.

I admire the restraint here, the poet's refusal to weigh in on her speakers. Her withholding of judgment resonates disturbingly with her speakers' ambiguous relationship to culpability. Things just happen, Elkins implies, and they often enough happen randomly, for no more reason than whatever reason we choose to assign to them— which itself is what, also random? Idiosyncratic? Who decides?

Reading these poems, I think of the photographs of Diane Arbus. I think, too, of the work of Frank Bidart, his early persona poems

that presented us with characters like Herbert White, a serial killer
with a soul of sorts. Both Arbus and Bidart give us what I think of
as presentation pieces: "Here," they seem to say, "this too is the
world; these people also live in and define it. Make of all of this
whatever you will." The poetry of *Blue Yodel* is not easy. It presents
uncomfortable truths and leaves us to wrestle with them on our own.
In the course of that wrestling, we learn a lot about what we know
versus what we'd prefer not to know; we pitch our beliefs against
those parts of the world that test our beliefs by resisting them.
We learn the limitations of belief, which is to say we confront the
limitation of self, of our ever fully being able to know a self—our
own, any more than another's:

> Unleash
> the wild animal that you are.
> Unbury yourself.
> ("Hunter's Moon")

Perhaps more easily said than done. Or maybe the doing is less
the problem; it's more an issue of being able—and willing—to
understand what we end up seeing when the self appears unleashed,
unburied, in front of us. This explains, I believe, the several
references to mirrors throughout *Blue Yodel*:

> All this time I saw the wolf
> in other men . . .

But when at last I looked into the moon
what met my gaze was the mirrored
wolf in me.

("Crying Wolf")

And, from "War Mask," in which courtship takes on a martial cast:

I couldn't recognize which hunter I was.
There are no mirrors

in war. I thought I was Achilles.
Then, Hector.

I was two enemies at once.

And then there's this passage, where a boy and the dead boy he's
found in a silo suddenly seem indistinguishable from one another:

I awoke in the deep night—
the boy was in the mirror
singing to himself.
By the moon's light
his two silver eyes
looked into mine.

("Aiming a Shotgun at the Sky")

True self-recognition may be one of the most challenging things to attain, inasmuch as it has to include much that we'd rather not see, the damage we've caused, the evil (whatever that may be) of which we're capable, irreversible regrets . . . Not all of the poems here involve self-reflection on the speaker's part. But I find that *Blue Yodel*, as a collection, presents us with situations whose questions become catalysts for self-reflection. "[H]uman kind/Cannot bear very much reality," as Eliot says; but trying to bear it, and for a time succeeding, is surely part of what contributes to the peculiar grace of stamina. This grace of stamina is what our essential poets have always provided. And it is among the many gifts of *Blue Yodel*, a book that reminds us that gifts can be tricky; they give us pleasure, but pleasure brings with it the power to disarm: at any moment, the world—what we thought was the world—may shift. In the poems of Ansel Elkins, beautifully, eerily, it does.

Carl Phillips

Blue Yodel

Blues for the Death of the Sun

The evening sun descended with the decorum of an old man
Who removes his wide-brimmed hat as a funeral march passes.
August. The rivers rose. We saw the sun vanish.
Like crows, the people of my town pace the streets, faces skyward.
From wet ground ferns spring, fronds greening with hunger.
The river reeks of gasoline burning in her current.
Across the blackened hills I hear a peacock holler his blue yodel.
Your hands ain't wings, a passing stranger tells me.
The sky has taken away light.
Is it punishment? the newspapers ask. *We thought God was dead.*
The newspaper printed this as if God could read.
I stand here waiting for something to happen.
An empty glass soda bottle rolls down the road.
The live oak's leaves seem to fatten with every passing minute.
I watched as the people of my town tore down a man
with their bare hands. They say he stole the light with his curse,
But I only thought he was talking to himself.
I ask the sky, *How come your hands left us?*
How does the ocean feel about no light? How quiet is her bell.
My people in the streets, calling. Their drowned faces.
A people, a piano, can't live without light.
People say that even if we go to the top of the mountain,
Even then we can't reach the light.
Our sky, bereft. Our heartmuscle, lit into blue flame.
We gnaw for light that lies beneath our skin.
We've turned to flames
Like a house burning itself from the inside out.

Goat Man

Like a bearded prophet out of the Old Testament
he travels through our county roads on foot
with his iron-wheeled wagon drawn by a herd
of thirty goats, the solitary music of trembling
tinware, beaten pails and kettles.
In the slash pine, children gather to see
him preach the Gospel. He lectures on God,
politics, and women. He says he was in Alabama
last week, and warns of the coming
race wars. Afterward he sold us postcards,
let us pet a newborn kid before we left for home.
In winter nights the goats sleep close; he heats
his supper over a fire of burning tires
and reads *Robinson Crusoe* in the intimate field
of light afforded by a kerosene lamp.
He nails his hand-painted sign to a live oak
by the roadside: GOD IS NOT DEAD. He rises
at first bird when the sun surfaces behind a hill.
We can hear the sound of bells carried
by his goats, their curved regal horns
breaking a path through the morning chill
of the Old Dixie highway where he walks
on the fresh-laid tar of the mid-twentieth century.

Mississippi Pastoral

1955

August: cotton blooms.
A brutal, feral laugh
spooks the mules.

Listen: sparrows
in the rail yard quietly
build nests; one

finds a broken bone-
china teacup by the tracks
and weaves hay within.

August. In this land, lost
things just happen
to be found. In the sky

a buzzard eyes a trapped rabbit
he's waited for. Scouring
the waist-high river grasses of

the Tallahatchie, a heat-dazed
sheriff removes his hat, shields
his blue eyes from the merciless sun.

He strides down the fishermen's path
with labored breath and gargantuan weight;
sweat soaks his white shirt, suspenders

mark a black X in the heat's sickly
embrace. Halting by the riverbank
he heaves, wrestles open

the buttons of his shirt collar to breathe.
Someone in a boat hollers
Over here, Sheriff. We found that nigger boy.

A seventy-five pound
cotton gin fan
strung with barbed wire

leashed to the child's neck. Swollen
August sun, white blaze. Today
the cotton fields set themselves on fire.

The River's Wife

When the lightkeeper's daughter heard God
say she would conceive a child
by wading out into the river alone,

she awoke in the deep heart
of humid midnight, the crescent
of sweat beneath her breasts soaking

her nightgown. She feared the indifference
in God's omen; she couldn't discern
whether it was punishment or a promise.

What if my child, she asked, *is fathered
by the Old Devil River himself?*—famed
as a watery lover so jealous he never let go

of a man with his clothes on. No other
river was this deceptive. Men who dared
to swim across the Mississippi rarely

took a bride. In summers we wade
into the wide lower river to baptize
our children and sing them free

of sin. A vigilant man,
her father said, *We must devote ourselves
to the light above.* His only daughter

watched as he kept the coal-oil lamp
burning for the barges and the steamboat
captains who navigated the innavigable

faithless waters. But when the river rose
last fall, it took her father with it.
She was heavy with the baby when she buried

him and repeated his words, *Keep the river
light burning.* In winter she bore a son
as fitful as his father. And every Sunday

after we sang our Savior's hymns,
she climbed to the top of the lighthouse
to be that much nearer.

The Girl with Antlers

I tore myself out of my own mother's womb.
There was no other way to arrive in this world.
A terrified midwife named me Monster
and left me in the pine woods with only the moon.
My mother's blood dripped from my treed head.

In a dream my mother came to me and said
if I was to survive
I must find joy within my own wild self.

When I awoke I was alone in solitude's blue woods.

                    *   *   *

A woman found me and took me to her mountain home
high at the end of an abandoned logging road.
We spent long winter evenings by the fire;
I sat at the hearth as she read aloud myths of the Greeks
while the woodstove roared behind me.
She sometimes paused to watch the wall of shadows
cast by my antlers. The shadows danced
across the entire room like an oak's wind-shaken branches.

                    *   *   *

The woman was worried when I would not wear dresses.
I walked naked through the woods.
She hung the wash from my head
on hot summer days when I sat in the sun to read.

The woman grew worried when I would not shed
my crown with the seasons as the whitetails did.
"But I am not a whitetail," I said.

*　*　*

When I became a woman
in the summer of my fifteenth year,
I found myself
suddenly changed in the mirror.
My many-pronged crown had grown
into a wildness all its own;
highly stylized, the bright
anarchic antlers were majestic to my eye.

The woman saw me and smiled. "What you are I cannot say,
but nature has created you.
You are fearfully and wonderfully made."

When night came it brought a full moon.
I walked through the woods to the lake
and knelt in the cool grass on its bank.
I saw my reflection on the water,
I touched my face.
You are fearfully and wonderfully made.

Adventures of the Double-Headed Girl

We are indeed a strange people

wedded together, axis of a shared spine

behind bifocals, scientists examine us

lusus naturae—our name penciled into a catalogue

enthralled, gentlemen wonder

might I possess two women at once?

arriving at a fork in the road, a man

will pull at his whiskers, ponder the possibilities,

and decide shrewdly *yes, 'tis better*

to slaughter two doves with his single stone

the fire-eater winks at us knowingly

is he flirting with me or you?

I reply with a kiss blown

from my tight-gloved hand

lettered men haven't printed the word

for this braided pleasure

two women corseted together

whet the spectators' appetite

like boys in front of a sweetshop window

the crowd of men in derby hats

jostle for a closer view of us

two women corseted together

the unspeakable, we are

a winged seed

Autobiography of Eve

Wearing nothing but snakeskin
boots, I blazed a footpath, the first
radical road out of that old kingdom
toward a new unknown.
When I came to those great flaming gates
of burning gold,
I stood alone in terror at the threshold
between Paradise and Earth.
There I heard a mysterious echo:
my own voice
singing to me from across the forbidden
side. I shook awake—
at once alive in a blaze of green fire.

Let it be known: I did not fall from grace.

I leapt
to freedom.

Winter Burial

St. Mary's Asylum for Girls, 1861

She cries in the snow.
In the freezing night I hear her echo,
faint, arriving like a whisper through the walls.
In our iron bed beneath wool
quilts, I touch Maria's ankle with my foot
to wake her. I tell her about the blood orange
I stole from a black preacher's coat.
This winter the rains wouldn't let up,
the sisters wouldn't let us out of doors.
We stayed inside, played by the windows, and wished
the gentleman with the high black silk hat
would come again riding on his horse.
But the rains didn't let up, and we buried our music
teacher in the school cemetery
and sang for her once more
before they laid her in the deep mud.
One eye open, she lay in her pine box
while we cried with the cold rain in our dresses.
It's snowing now. The bell's midnight toll
ripples into the freezing night and I
peel open the orange. *Maria,* I whisper.
Pray for your mama—the Creole whore
who you call for relentlessly in your sleep.
I was a ghost to my mother too.
I can't recall her face, but she returns to me

in winter dreams when I wait to be buried
beneath the hoarfrost. We lie awake and listen
for the shadow man with the high black hat
to come riding through the season of snow and ice
on a horse named Violence.

Coffin Bone

to a rider thrown from a horse

You had been warned
Not to venture near the unnamed
Colt no rider had yet broken.
But you chose him,
Admired the white blaze
Across his face,
His litheness,
His muscles only a god
Could fashion.
Rider, yet still you approached his stall
Whistling, offered a handful of sweet feed,
Courted him with
The season's brightest apple.
The other men grew quiet as you bridled him;
The colt's murderous
Eye darkened, his nostrils flared.
The other men said, *He'll bury you*
In the wind.
Like an archer
Stringing his final bow on the battlefield,
You drew tight the reins,
Lit bareback out of the barn.
Set this field on fire,
You urged as you and he became
The bluest flame within the body

Of speed. The second hand's stroke
Knows only to devour the burning
Wheel of the clock.
Even God dared not
Break the rider from the ride.
You chose the field.
You chose the horse.
Goddamn you, you chose the horse.

Devil's Rope

after the old-time ballad "Ruby," by Cousin Emmy

I uncurl your fist as you sleep, Ruby.
The slow sound of your breath; the house is still. At dawn
the deer move like ghosts over the hill, trailed by that devil,
the patient wolf. I open your hand and cover it with mine.
Will you forgive me, love, when you're buried
beyond the sun's reach, beyond the dark brothers?

Our preacher told it like thunder, "All my good brothers,
should the snake tempt you with his wet ruby
tongue, should sin take root within you, buried
in the dark cavern of your heart, know this: God made dawn
for redemption. God whispered into this ear of mine:
'When men fall into desire, they fall into the arms of the devil.'"

In my own dreams I battle with the devil.
He and I could be blood brothers.
He leads me into the ground, down a pitch-black mine,
guides my hand over an earthen wall that spells your name, Ruby.
I touch the ember letters, leave my hand to bear the heat. Dawn
be damned, I will remain here, buried.

I killed our ancient blue rooster and buried
his singing beak in the garden while you slept, before that devil
could disturb your slumber to report that dawn
has arrived here in the cold hills of Old Brothers

Mountain. I saved you the cockscomb, the fancy ruby
cap he prized. But the blades of his spurs are mine.

The men said I couldn't keep a woman restless as mine.
Making a wife of her, they said, is like trying to bury
the wind. And even barbed wire can't fence in the wind, Ruby.
Winter: the secret reddening of your cheeks where the devil
kissed his crimson prayer. Men broke the mouths of their brothers
battling for you. Only scattered blood remains in the hay at dawn.

I welcome the early light breaking through the Appalachian dawn,
take the spade from my tool chest, head to dig in Brown's coal mine.
I will turn loose the colts from the barn; I will curse my brothers
that we ever drank from the cold spring's wicked water buried
in the loneliest ground. I drank from the clawed hand of the devil;
I whispered your name into the mountain peaks, Ruby.

The devil's rosined bow begins to fiddle at dawn
as his brothers pick banjo. I carve your name in the stump below
    mine.
I'll sing for you, Ruby, and lay you in the shade where the rooster's
    buried.

Baby Doll

You left early this morning: white bloomers
Blowing on the clothesline,
The chores undone, the broom
Leaning against your mama's unpainted porch
While you roam down the red dirt road
Lazily whistling
In a dusty pair of Mary Janes
And a white unbuttoned dress
That stirs up jealousy
Among the field hands,
Who follow you with their huntsmen's eyes;
They say you the finest little filly in the field
But surly as a colt.
At seventeen you've begun
To gaze far past the blazing
Sweep of cotton
Fields and honey-talking
Men who'd burn up the barn
For your hand. And I too
Dream that some day soon
I'll fly my crop duster
High above the power lines,
Spray kaolin dust over those wily suitors,
Sweep you beyond the autumn
Fields and over the river
Into womanhood.

Tennessee Williams on Art and Sex

At the time I was writing "Battle of Angels" and . . . The crowded avenue of umbrellas and passersby hailing cabs in the rain makes it difficult to hear. *What did you say?* I ask. *I said it was a period of loneliness*, you shout. The subject is promiscuity. Men in gray suits and hats leap gracefully over a water-swollen grate. Through a fine curtain of rain, streets sing with gray light. *What I love about this city are the pigeons*, you say. *The way things can be so fucking rotten, yet they sleep together under the eaves of cathedrals and brothels. They keep warm that way.*

It's unavoidable—a piercing, fleeting scent of other people's bodies. Strange how the heat and sweat of skin mixes with rain. Beneath gray wide-open wings of a newspaper, a woman shields herself. You stop at a corner bodega to light a cigarette, lean against a crate of oranges. *Tell me again about desire and writing.* But you don't hear me. From a third-floor apartment a woman's cry rings out. She's having a heated telephone conversation in the tub. Rising wisps of steam escape the window where she hangs her bare legs. *Then goodbye, Henry*, she says. From the open window, her naked feet are like two strangers
facing each other.

Real Housewives

Gossip is the last great oral tradition.
    —Grace Paley

The best gossip begins like kindling
    ignited and fanned to flame.
        Rising out of the ashes
of a divorce, her life in foreclosure,
    the housewife must reauthor herself:
        she unzips the old skin and begins anew
under the knife of a celebrity surgeon
    reputed to be shrewd. Voilà! She resurfaces
        post-surgery with lips ballooned.
At a dinner party from hell, one wife
    sidelines another wife: *Why were you alone*
        with my husband? The night
is suddenly electric. Tragedy
    is two women trapped within
        the eternal return of the same
cocktail dress. The wives weave
    felicitous texts upon a theme
        of vaginaplasty
after the pageantry of the baby
    bump, pregnant in heels.
        Now there's talk
of the It Girl
    whose boob job on live TV
        has gone woefully awry. OMG,

the tête-à-tête of misaligned titties:
    adventures in surgery
        left her with a pair of unsynchronized swimmers.
The glitterati say the only thing worse
    than being blogged about
        is *not* being blogged about.
The wives fawn over the tawdry tweeted
    snark, pleased to read
        of the airing out of a mistress's dirty
string-thong bikini. *Ladies! We've enough*
    white wine to go around. Between the sweet tinkling
        of tall-stemmed, sugar-rimmed glasses
and a chorus of chitchatting ex-wives,
    a villainista eagle-eyes
        her rival across a dinner table; deliciously
plotting, she tears into a bleeding tenderloin
    with her bright teeth, encircles the Other Woman
        in her sniper's crosshairs,
and with *furor loquendi*
    Pearl Harbors her enemy:
        You need to close your legs to married men.
A terrorista hurls a Molotov cocktail
    in the shape of a pink martini
        as emery-boarded claws surface to air
with vengeance. There is girl-on-girl
    action, there's a woman threatening to release
        a night-vision sex tape to the paparazzi.

And now a close-up money shot
    of a blonde: high-volume teased hair, hot-pink
        lipsticked lips agape upon
viewing the red-hot, six-inch-long
    stiletto her rival unhooves,
        wielding it as a weapon.
Brava! Climax. Shoegasm. *Finish her!* shouts
    one who obviously never heard of finishing school.
        All the weeklies will moralize
how it's all fun and games
    until someone's husband hangs
        himself. At home
the injured wife ices her wound with a Bloody
    Mary to the rescue. She fronts the mirror,
        touches up her blush, embalms her lips
to match the living
    room walls, gunmetal
        gray. Each day
adds a new pearl
    to the necklace
        of betrayals.
She stares into her mirrored face—a farce
    of a cry pantomimed, a comedy
        more Chaplinesque than burlesque—
she speaks into the mirror, which speaks
    into the camera, and in turn to our TV:
        I'm not here to make friends.

Monogamy

After the workweek we
undress and have celebratory sex
that lasts as long as a mint on the tongue.
Habitually, my husband
inhales the familiar musk of my hair
and dozes. October light
leaves sooner now. Shadows
stretch through the rooms, swallow
the amber light as I listen
to the tiny ticking of my husband's
wristwatch, the migration of wild
geese calling relentlessly
southward, to lands where the sun
warms the eternally green
trees, where a woman bathes in the sea
alone, drifting and anonymous.
She's nobody's wife. White-crested
waves swell but never break
at the shore.
Outside my window, the crying V of geese
bleeds away into another city.
In the bedroom, a sudden
vague yet putrid smell from the vase
of expired chrysanthemums, yellowed
and irretrievable,
by the western bay window.

The Lighthouse Keeper

I aimed a rock at the back of the angel's head
and hit him. He fell. That evening
I found him at the old harbor,
tangled in the electric lines;
his left wing was burnt: in the night air
an acrid stink of feathers.
I bound his hands with fisherman's rope,
hefted him into the bed of my pickup,
and drove along the coastal highway home.

*   *   *

I open a beer and wait
for the angel to awaken.
When I stroke his wings
they release
a silken shimmer of mica-like dust onto my fingers
like what remains
after you catch hold of a moth,
feel its tiny fury of wings battling
within your pinned hands.

*   *   *

The sleeping angel's naked body
is a marvel, — his copper skin
sun-darkened from flying.

Is this skybound feral boy
the sun's sole child?
What if he's half-human, half-wild —
the bastard child of God? Exiled
from the afterworld? Or escaped
as Icarus?
Like a muddy oyster shucked,
the pearls of his eyes
open; — but no pupils,
only two gray orphans
like a compass
without a magnetic field.

                    *   *   *

If God wants his angel back
He'll have to come claim him Himself.

And so I chain the angel to the radiator
and begin to build a cage by the window.

                    *   *   *

Each day I bring the angel honey from wild bees. I sing
the only song my mother ever sang to me:

     Mama's little baby love shortnin', shortnin',
     Mama's little baby love shortnin' bread.

He licks the honey from my open hand;
thrill of his lion's hot tongue
muscling between the slats of his cage.

                    *   *   *

At dawn the angel watches the fishermen depart
in battered boats. Wings spread wide
as a buzzard's
he suns himself by the window
and keeps ceaseless watch
over the empty harbor at low tide,
the sky absent of all but the crying
gulls as they coast on invisible wind.

Tornado

When the sky threw down hail, I knew
    our world was sudden, changing. In the violence of rains
        we ran. I held my daughter with her water-soaked braids.
She covered her ears and counted
    one Mississippi, two Mississippi
        the space between lightning and thunder.
We heard sirens. Birds fled the sky. Soon
    the wick of the world smelled matchstick blue.
        three Mississippi, four
When the winds had blown off all the doors
    we were soldered only by a handhold.
        I'm not a believer
but I took shelter inside a prayer
    when I saw a white horse
        fly across the sky.
one Mississippi, two
    I tried to tether you
        to me. Through sweeping winds
of glass and debris
    I struggled to see.
        one—
I watched my daughter fly away
    from the grapnel of my arms. Unmoored,
        like a skiff she sailed alone out the window.
I awoke into the fingertips of rain
    light against my face. Wreckage
        of a new world greeted me—

a pink bicycle lodged in an oak tree,
  bright spoke beads in the shape of stars
    on a wheel still spinning.

Aiming a Shotgun at the Sky

I

My mother spoke less as winter wore on.

Winter had settled into her knees, she said.
Seated by the woodstove, she combed
her coal-black hair, watched the snow
rush at the curtainless window.
January seemed inescapable.

II

I took my father's shotgun
into the stilled woodland. I listened
for quail. Above, the sound of falling
leaves through naked limbs. It began
to snow again. How alone
the woods were as I roamed the quiet
clear-cut field where deer graze. In falling snow
I heard the field singing.
   I play here for hours in the abandoned silos
   when no one knows where I am.
Here, I peered into each silo, the open
roofs long since crumbled in; I spoke my name
into each hollow, listened to the echo

pitch back a voice not quite my own.
I reached the last silo and there, lying inside, was a boy
who looked as if he was sleeping
inside a canoe. He was missing
his left hand, cleanly severed. His mouth,
when I touched it, felt like a songbird
fallen out of a frozen nest. I found
a gray-black feather glazed in ice
and lay it over his lips. The wind
blew snow over his open eyes.

He seemed to keep a secret
inside the deep pocket of his body.
I listened for him to tell it.

Blackbird, I said, *I will sing to you*
so you won't feel alone.
The quiet field, covered with snow, was falling asleep.

III

My father returned with the hunters—
they hung a buck from the oak outside our house:
his hind legs spread, hung upside down,
carcass cooling,

a stick propped between
his ribs. The beast
hung for days in the tree.

   I V

I unlaced the boy's shoes, his stiff feet locked in gray socks.
I replaced them with my own
boots, tied his leather laces into bows.

   v

By the woodstove, my mother
drew a fine-tooth comb through her
black hair threaded with sudden silver.

She stared into the fire
until her face burned on one side.

The room felt emptier with my mother in it.

VI

I awoke in the deep night—
the boy was in the mirror
singing to himself.
By the moon's light
his two silver eyes
looked into mine.

VII

Winter nights grew moonless. Father
was splitting winter wood
with his axe

while snow fell like ashes
over black oaks.

VIII

At dusk the woods fell asleep in the snow.
I followed the fox's path to the silent field
but at the silo
. . . nothing. Only snow.

I called and called him home,
searched into the snowing sky
who hid him inside its gray coat of wool.
But the sky was a deaf-mute; it gave no reply.
And the empty field only buried
itself deep beneath the ceaseless snow.
  Would winter ever end? Would trees of ice
  ever thaw?

I left one red glove in the snow
and headed home.

Hour of the Wolf

3 a.m.

Who is awake but the night watchman?
Or the grim laborer in the graveyard
Shift? The spirit world is in transit —

Souls of the newdead drift
Like floating lanterns
Over a river woven with ghosts.

Somewhere at the crossroads of night
A man will come to the vanishing line
Of his life. All the world he's known

Closes into a clock of smoke;
In that final unannullable hour
The self is torn from time and calendar:

Mind undresses from body,
Its clothes of blood and bone.
As it crosses through the door of death

The spirit reaches the lips of the unknown
And sings
Through it: —
                    Newborn

Into nothingness,
Mind floats through starlight
Like an oarless boat along the coastline.

What is *ghost*
But the echo of a man
As he roams his native hills and roads and home?

He wears the mist
In his hair,
His voice: the hounds of wind.

This veil
Between the living and the dead
Is smoke-thin

Here in the wrecking hour of deep night
Where we lie awake and listen
For the white wolf to arrive.

Reverse: A Lynching

Return the tree, the moon, the naked man
Hanging from the indifferent branch
Return blood to his brain, breath to his heart
Reunite the neck with the bridge of his body
Untie the knot, undo the noose
Return the kicking feet to ground
Unwhisper the word *jesus*
Rejoin his penis with his loins
Resheathe the knife
Regird the calfskin belt through trouser loops
Refasten the brass buckle
Untangle the spitting men from the mob
Unsay the word *nigger*
Release the firer's finger from its trigger
Return the revolver to its quiet holster
Return the man to his home
Unwidow his wife
Unbreak the window
Unkiss the crucifix of her necklace
Unsay *Hide the children in the back*, his last words
Repeal the wild bell of his heart
Reseat his family at the table over supper
Relace their fingers in prayer, unbless the bread
Rescind the savagery of men
Return them from animal to human, reborn in the long run
Backward to the purring pickup
Reignite the Ford's engine, its burning headlights

Retreat down the dirt road, tires speeding
Backward into rising dust
Backward past cornfields, past the night-floating moths
Rescind the whiskey from the guts
Unswallowed, unswigged, the tongue unstung
Rehouse the flask in the field coat's interior pocket
Unbare the teeth, unwhet the appetite
Return the howl to its wolf
Return the shovel to the barn, the rope to the horse's stable
Resurrect the dark from its heart housed in terror

Reenter the night through its door of mercy

Crying Wolf

All this time I saw the wolf
in other men: cavern-eyed,
famished with winter, moon-white teeth
blood-streaked,
devouring the elk while its heart still beat.
I swore I could see
the wolf in other men.
But when at last I looked into the moon
what met my gaze was the mirrored
wolf in me.

Mississippi Delta: Glass in the Field

I've found the woman I will marry, he said.

Had we been playing chess I would have held the queen
motionless above the board, readying her coy move
into the feudal geometry, the bloodred
square where his knight waited.

But we were only stationed at scarred barstools beneath a haze of blue
neon lights, a veil of cigarette smoke, the background noise
of other people's voices.

I've found the woman I will marry.

Had I continued to look at his face,
white queens would have fallen from my mouth.

     *   *   *

We walked to my front door as evening spread her grand indigo
gown across the town.
This was midsummer. His mouth
made melody of the words *Tennessee*
and *she*. The music
of her name lit the night
like a sparkler.

     *   *   *

Deep in the heart of the delta: a wide endless ribbon
of highway; a pickup's northbound headlights
break the blackness. Other
than the road that leads to Memphis
there's nothing here
but soybean fields begging to be watered.

I sleep naked, the open window
of my rented bedroom with its torn screen
invites a drift of winged nocturnal
insects. A moth flutters giant blind wings
against my ear. Suddenly
breaking from sleep, I ask aloud

Who killed all the horses in the field?

War Mask

When I undressed you I discovered
a portrait of your ex

tattooed across your back, her auburn hair
painted as waves of flame, her name

a petroglyph in the lithic skin
on your shoulder blade. Men

hunt in straight lines, arrow-like.
Women set nets, deceitful lines laced by hook and eye.

It's a foxhunt in full cry,
a pack of hounds with galloping horses

and their scarlet-coated riders in pursuit.
Courtship is a blood sport.

I searched for you through the battlefield's smoke
and found you in ruins. I wove

my hands through your black hair
mixed with blood and branches.

I couldn't recognize which hunter I was.
There are no mirrors

in war. I thought I was Achilles.
Then, Hector.

I was two enemies at once.

Thou Shalt Not

No *don't*, no law
No law, no lock
No lock, no key
No key, no discovery
No discovery, no sin
No sin, no guilt
No guilt, no deceit
No deceit, no mask
No mask, no fright
No fright, no delight
No delight, no devil
No devil, no night
No night, no tiger
No tiger, no hunt
No hunt, no game
No game, no chase
No chase, no catch
No catch, no kill
No kill, no thrill
No thrill, no thrust
No thrust, no lust
No lust, no lay
No lay, no lies
No lies, no hide
No hide, no seek
No seek, no snake
No snake, no Eve

No Eve, no Fall
No Fall, no man
No man, no you
No you, no *yes*.

The Call of the Wild

The difference between you and other men
is the difference
between wolf and dog.

I could smell it on you
all the way across a crowded room.
(Speech isn't all it's cracked up to be.)

I felt the midsummer moon on my skin.
I felt my scarlet dress was on fire.

It was as if I had the bone buried in my body

and I wanted you
to use everything but your hands
to find it.

Every line out of my mouth is a lie
except the one that begins with *I want*.

Between your teeth
is where I want to be.

I tried to be good, I tried to be civilized;

but the body's unbridled
appetite
lured me like a hunter into the animal night.

Resisting you
was like trying to hide from the moon.

Werewolf in a Girls' Dormitory

The Reformatory School for Misbehaving Girls
keeps its young vixens walled in.

Keep out of the woods, warns the headmistress.

The girls hear a howling in the distance.

Beware a gray-coated man who walks the road alone
on a snowy night; he wears the brim of his hat low.

Though miles away, he catches a trace of your sweet scent
            —and follows it.

Lycanthropy 101: Educated young ladies must learn
to recognize a seducer
                            by his moonrise eyes.

            *   *   *

Behind the courtyard, a redheaded schoolgirl in a plaid skirt
leans against an apple tree, secretly smoking
and reading a banned novel.

        She's wayward . . . in all the right ways.

Nightfall—
the redhaired girl climbs out her window and runs through moonlight

into the night woods, where she whispers
Wolf! Come find me.

Going to the Movies Alone

Tonight, I want to see something explode.
I want to see a dirty blonde
in a ripped white tank
pointing a gun at a bald man
who looks like me.
I want to see a lot less talk and a lot more action.
I want to watch a powerful man be seduced
by the wrong woman.
I want to see someone start believing in Jesus.
I want to see someone baptized
in blood and bullets and gore and gunfire.
I want to see an expensive woman in a diamond bikini
light a stick of dynamite and dive into the sea.
I want to tear through the border between dream and reality.
I want to see the American beast unleashed
in suburbia, see citizens fleeing the uncaged
monster as he storms through our city.
I want a high body count and screaming
police sirens in the chase scene.
I want to see a bomb blown on-screen in 3D.
I want to feel the flame and debris,
hear the blood-smeared Superfather say to his son,
"Everything's gonna be OK. We won."
I want to see the sun rise once again over the burnt city
before the theater lights come on
and I go out the door marked EXIT
and into the winter night, the vast

dark parking lot slick with snow and ice
where my car waits alone under a streetlight.
I clear the frost from my window,
try to unlock the frozen door.

On Leaving the Boy in the Battlefield

after Archilochus

Your harsh mare faces the wind   she moves against
The soldiers left me in the field with   you, staunching
The wound of your neck   my brother, my twin
I know it's you by your dagger   your sharp penis
You ate raw honey from the beehive   & I, as usual
Watched the bees crawl on your lips   beneath the pine I'll situate you
I'll bury your head in the honeycomb   Melisseus will be sufficed
When they hear the news, the women will hang red sheets   in the city
Since you've died without a face, you're a kite   & therefore you imagine
Me roaming the streets naked, calling your name   we establish beauty.

Ghost at My Door

When my daughter disappeared, the town gathered
to search the frozen river.

Her name was read on the radio,
printed on milk cartons
and the front page of the county newspaper.

I found no trace of her. Nothing
but the succession of hours,
dumb, numberless, indifferent.
Sleepless, I hollered across the hills
her name, the name I chose for the music
of its two simple syllables. The birds
in the trees have memorized my call.
They repeat her name, return it to me in song.

———

Near an abandoned sawmill by the river
the search party unearthed the woven rope
bracelet she'd worn that day.
The sheriff brought it to me in a plastic ziplock bag.
He found tire tracks by the unpaved road
alongside the river. Sunk into mud and snow,
a heavy bootprint.

The boot sole left little Xs in the mud.

JANUARY

I dreamt that I'd uncover her sleeping
face in the ground like Snow White
shepherded by kindly dwarves.
I combed through the woods and slash
pine in unlaced boots.
I called her name
and called her name.
Was God so cruel?

I, too, became unlaced.

FEBRUARY

All this time I haven't cried.
The women in the supermarket cry for me.

MARCH

I gathered all the dresses—mine *and* hers—
and burned them in a pile in the yard.

I left the wire hangers to hang in the empty closet
because they wouldn't burn.

———

The only clothes I own are those my father left behind.
My arms inhabit the sleeves of his field coat, its lining torn.
I loved how his hands smelled of sweet feed
when he came back from the barn in evenings.

He liked to be alone
when he walked every morning at sunrise.

I would go to the window of our cabin and watch him
head down the road with his cane until he vanished behind the hill.

APRIL

Her teacher came by to bring the rest of her things.
Her red raincoat with a strand of hair still in its hood.
The contents of its pocket: a candy wrapper, a dime,
a piece of string for cat's cradle.
And a small, stapled handmade booklet
titled in green crayon *My book of seasons.*
On the left page was penciled *Fall.*

> *Five fat turkeys are we.*
> *We slept all night in the tree.*
> *Till the cook came*
> *around, we couldn't be found,*
> *and that's why we're here, you see!*

On the facing page she illustrated the fat birds
safely perched on the tree's high stretched arm.

And then *Spring*.

> *I am like spring. I like to jump rope.*
> *Spring is the season for flying kites.*
> *Hello, my mother sees me fly my good kite.*

And I was reminded of that past April, how the sun
sang to the land as it leaned at the edge of ripening
season. Wind swept through the greening
limbs, muscled through the budding tulip trees.
She built a kite, fashioned the sail
out of an old scarlet dress I discarded.
I watched her from the kitchen window while I washed dishes.
She flew it across the field, the kite's
scarlet sail hurrying skyward. My daughter
fed the line through her bare fingers
and called out to me to come see
how she could make it dance in the air like a flaming bird.

MAY

I tore the front door from its hinge
and threw it in the pasture.
What was the use of keeping anyone out or in?

JUNE

———

JULY

———

AUGUST

———

SEPTEMBER

Nothing lives here anymore. Only hushed land.
Cinder blocks. A bicycle tire. Shards
of mirror gleam from the muddy yard.
Stained glass in the gravel road. I shattered
all the windows. This house
held sorrows too heavy
for any one woman to hold.

OCTOBER

Fog rolls over the pasture, weaves through open windows.
Stationed at the dilapidated porch
I smoke my father's pipe,
cradle its warm wood bowl
in my graying hand.

I took a pocket knife, severed my long braid,
and threw it in the yard.
The following morning it was gone.
I dreamt a wolf
crept to my cabin by night and stole it.

NOVEMBER

I watch the rising breath of the half-starved mare
as she stands in bare, frozen field,
too hungry to move, even though I've left
the pasture gate open
and wait for her to leave.

DECEMBER

The mare is finally gone from the field.

The crows too have left the trees.
Rolling fog reaches across pasture.
Wind guides its fingers into the windowless
house, threads through the yawn of absent
door, where, even if nothing inside
me moves, the wind's breath
moves through *me*. Sings
through my bones like wind chimes
hanging from eaves. Awakens
my skin to the forgotten sense of touch.
And I remember I am still alive
in the world of the living
where a spider has quietly
made herself my companion,
her web extravagantly spun
within the gulf of window frame.

From here I see a bird
at the top branch of the tulip tree begin
to clean gray wings.

——

I wonder why not even her ghost has returned
though I wait for her
at the door of the physical world.

Hunter's Moon

She cannot hide
her line of footprints in the snow.
The trail leads from her window—
across the blank page of winter
field, across the barbed wire
fence and its posted sign that says *No
Trespassing*, across the night's
quiet deer path—and ends at his barn door.
At this late hour her only witness
is the private eye of
the moon, which hides
its voluminous histories of human
secrets—hers,

         and ours, too.
There is nothing between us
but the night. The hunter's appetite
is instinct; it dwells deep
and urges you: Unleash
the wild animal that you are.

        Unbury yourself.

Long Hungry Road

The horses remember the way
and at last we arrive at the other side
of the mountain. Blood of other men

stained into our bootlaces. I ride my last
Appaloosa, Big Man. A long knife
scar across his mouth.

A man who doesn't speak
lurches home alongside me
on a stolen, starved mare;

I helped dig his brother's grave.
Strapped atop the pannier
is his youngest son, fallen

asleep against his father's back
to the rhythm of horses'
hooves stomping through char and rock and ash.

The jangle of Big Man's bridle and reins
is all the music I've salvaged —
and he won't make it much longer down the road.

Tomorrow, when my horse dies,
I'll leave him saddled. Before flies
congregate in his nostrils, I'll unearth

the buried silver bit from his mouth.
And when we reach the ruined town
with its name burned off the map,

the whipped faces of its inhabitants
will watch us with blood-black eyes.
All they'll say is *You survived.*

The mute man and his boy will disappear
down a different road to see what remains
of their folks back home on the coast.

And I'll keep on the road alone
past broken plows and smoking farmlands
until I find the sprawling live oak—

I'll nail to its trunk Big Man's bridle,
listen as the ghost of my horse
lives on as a wind chime

in the tree's giant limbs—outstretched,
ceaseless, green. When the musical wind
runs through the oak, it runs through me.

Sailmaker's Palm

My black-haired bride was made of sails.
She was a ship; her wedding sails were white.
I made her dress with yards of canvas.
Winding stitch after stitch, I sewed all night.

I was a child to the wind.
I listened to it like a father.
I put an inwardly spiraled shell to my ear
to hear what the sea had to say.

A web spun between weeds. Like a memory
I keep forgetting
of being kissed for the first time at the sea; —
her wind-whipped red hair, her bathing suit of cobalt blue.

What is memory but wind
blowing through you?

My bride was a full-rigged ship
being launched to sea. On her maiden voyage
she was thrown into the wild green Atlantic.

At the hour of my death
carry me to the graveyard by boat
as on Bequia, island of the cloud,
where the dead were ferried by oarsmen

who rowed *de dead stroke:*—
they took one stroke through water,
        then feathered the oars,
took the next stroke through the air,
        then feathered the oars.
The oarsmen of the island
transported both body and spirit
into the afterlife.

I saw my wife sailing beneath the light
of a full moon. Her bright sails illumined,
she rides across a ghostly topography.

The shipwright ran a ragged hand down the entire length
of the vessel's hull from stern to stem.
He looked up at the wooden figurehead—
bare breasted, her hair all around her.
Her wild blank eyes unpainted.

When a sailor dies at sea
the ship's sailmaker sews the dead man into a canvas shroud.
Stitch by stitch, the sailmaker closes him tightly round
with twine; he works his way from foot to head.
And the last stitch
he sews through the dead man's nose.

Death, Captain,
is not what I feared it would be.
I was blown through death.
Death blew through me.
I was sewn into the wind itself
as a singing voice blown out to sea.

Acknowledgments

Thank you to the editors of the following publications, in which some of these poems, sometimes in different versions, originally appeared:

AGNI: "Coffin Bone"
The American Scholar: "Adventures of the Double-Headed Girl," "The
    Girl with Antlers," "Monogamy," "Thou Shalt Not"
The Believer: "Tennessee Williams on Art and Sex"
Boston Review: "Reverse: A Lynching"
Copper Nickel: "Winter Burial"
Ecotone: "The Lighthouse Keeper"
Fugue: "Real Housewives"
Guernica: "Blues for the Death of the Sun"
Gulf Coast: "Mississippi Delta: Glass in the Field"
Heck: "Going to the Movies Alone"
Linebreak: "War Mask"
Mississippi Review: "Ghost at My Door"
Ninth Letter: "On Leaving the Boy in the Battlefield"
North American Review: "Mississippi Pastoral"
Ostrich Review: "Baby Doll"
Oxford American: "Tornado"
Parnassus: "Sailmaker's Palm"
The Southern Review: "Goat Man," "Devil's Rope"
Third Coast: "The River's Wife"

"Ghost at My Door" was reprinted in *Best New Poets 2011*, ed. D. A. Pow-
    ell (Charlottesville: University of Virginia Press, 2012).
"On Leaving the Boy in the Battlefield" was reprinted in *Poets & Writers*.
"Reverse: A Lynching" was reprinted online at the Writers' Corner, a sec-
    tion on the Web site of the National Endowment for the Arts featur-
    ing past and current literature fellows: http://arts.gov/writers-corner
    /bio/ansel-elkins.

I am deeply grateful to the following institutions and organizations
for their generous support and encouragement of my work: the National
Endowment for the Arts, the North Carolina Arts Council, the American
Antiquarian Society, Mystic Seaport Museum, Hedgebrook, the Bucknell

Seminar for Younger Poets, the Sewanee Writers' Conference, the Unterberg Poetry Center, *The Paris Review*, and the Standard East Village.

Many thanks to the marvelous teachers who have guided me, including Thomas Lux, Vijay Seshadri, Stuart Dischell, David Roderick, Linda Gregg, and especially Laure-Anne Bosselaar. Thanks to the poets, writers, and editors who encouraged me along the way: Nikky Finney, Cornelius Eady, Rebecca Gayle Howell, Vaughan Fielder, Ellie Burkey, Jonathan Morrow, Ricardo Maldonado, Timothy Donnelly, Bill Vollmann, Dominic Luxford, Lorin Stein, and Langdon Hammer. My deep gratitude to Carl Phillips for lifting this book into the light.

I am thankful for the wisdom of my dear friends and trusted guides: Yakini Kemp, Nzinga Kadalie Kemp, Jan Jenner, Herndon Dowling, David Yaffe, Donika Ross, Catherine Gilbert, Aaron Gilbreath, Amelie Welden, Chris Tobin, Thera Webb, Julie Henderson, and Kali Fajardo-Anstine.

My great gratitude to my family, who buoyed me with their love and support: Grandmama Maria Esther Peña, Marianna Rodriguez, Cecilia Barfield, Lauren Booker, Eva Mae Embry, Mary Gem Tidmore, Barbara Ann Zak, Betsy Carr, Revell Carr Sr., Geordie Carr, and Mieko Imai.

And finally, to Hilary Elkins and Keller Galvin and Revell Carr, whose love makes all things possible.

Printed and bound by CPI Group (UK) Ltd, Croydon, CR0 4YY

09/06/2025

14685978-0001